PST. WILLIAM HILLS

Godly Meditation And Inner Peace For Christians

A Guide Book For A Better Meditation

Copyright © 2024 by Pst. William hills

All rights reserved. No part of this publication may be reproduced, stored or transmitted in any form or by any means, electronic, mechanical, photocopying, recording, scanning, or otherwise without written permission from the publisher. It is illegal to copy this book, post it to a website, or distribute it by any other means without permission.

Pst. William hills asserts the moral right to be identified as the author of this work.

First edition

This book was professionally typeset on Reedsy. Find out more at reedsy.com

Contents

INTRODUCTION	1
CHAPTER 1	3
CHAPTER 2	8
CHAPTER 3	13
CHAPTER 4	19
CHAPTER 5	25
CHAPTER 6	31
CHAPTER 7	37
CHAPTER 8	43
CHAPTER 9	49
CHAPTER 10	55
CONCLUSION	62

INTRODUCTION

In a world that constantly demands our attention and fills our minds with noise and distraction, it has become increasingly difficult to find true peace and stillness. The never-ending stream of information, responsibilities, and worries can leave us feeling overwhelmed, anxious, and disconnected from the very source of our strength – our relationship with God.

As Christians, we are called to a life of peace, one that is grounded in our faith and trust in the Lord. However, too often we find ourselves caught up in the busyness of daily life, allowing our minds to be consumed by the stresses and pressures of this world. It is in these moments that the practice of godly meditation becomes a lifeline, a way to quiet our souls and reconnect with the unwavering love and presence of our Heavenly Father.

This book is a guide to rediscovering the profound peace that can only be found through a deep and intentional relationship with God. It is a journey into the practice of Christian meditation, a discipline that has been embraced by believers throughout the centuries as a way to draw closer to the Lord and experience the fullness of His peace.

Within these pages, you will find a comprehensive exploration of the biblical foundations for meditation, as well as practical strategies for incorporating this transformative practice into your daily life. We will delve into the art of meditating on God's Word, allowing the living truth of Scripture to penetrate our hearts and minds, and find solace in the promises of our faithful God.

Beyond the study of Scripture, we will also explore the power of prayer and praise as a form of meditation, inviting the presence of the Holy Spirit into our lives and cultivating an attitude of gratitude and worship. You will learn how to find peace in the midst of life's storms by resting in the unwavering love and sovereignty of our Heavenly Father.

Throughout our journey, we will address the practical challenges that often hinder our ability to find true inner peace, such as anxiety, worry, and the distractions of modern life. We will discover the transformative power of meditating on God's creation and the beauty of nature, allowing the wonders of the world around us to point us back to the majesty of our Creator.

Ultimately, this book is an invitation to experience the peace that surpasses all understanding, a peace that can only be found through a deep and abiding relationship with Christ. It is a call to surrender our burdens, our fears, and our restless minds to the One who promises to give us rest. Join me on this journey towards inner peace, a journey that will strengthen your faith, renew your spirit, and draw you ever closer to the loving embrace of our Heavenly Father.

CHAPTER 1

The Biblical Foundation for Meditation and Inner Peace

"You will keep in perfect peace all who trust in you, all whose thoughts are fixed on you!" - **Isaiah 26:3 NLT**

From the very beginning, the Bible has extolled the virtues of meditation as a pathway to peace, wisdom, and a deeper connection with God. This ancient spiritual practice, rooted in the teachings of Scripture, has been embraced by believers across generations as a means to quiet the mind, still the soul, and find rest in the unwavering promises of our Heavenly Father.

The concept of meditation permeates the pages of the Bible, woven into the stories of patriarchs, prophets, and even our Lord and Savior Jesus Christ. It is a discipline that invites us to set aside the noise and distractions of this world, and instead, to fix our thoughts on the eternal truths of God's Word and His unfailing love for us.

One of the earliest examples of meditation in the Bible can be found in the book of Genesis, where we are told that "Isaac went out to meditate in the field toward evening" (Genesis 24:63 NASB). Here, we see Isaac, the son of Abraham and heir to the covenant promises, taking time to reflect and commune with God in the solitude of nature. This simple act of meditation allowed him to find solace and strength in the midst of the challenges he faced, and to draw closer to the Lord who had called him.

Throughout the Psalms, we are repeatedly encouraged to meditate on the Word of God, to ponder His precepts, and to allow them to shape our thoughts and actions. In Psalm 1, the psalmist declares, "Blessed is the one... whose delight is in the law of the Lord, and who meditates on his law day and night" (Psalm 1:1-2 NIV). This passage reminds us that true blessing and fulfillment can be found by making the practice of meditating on God's Word a central part of our lives.

Prayer:

Heavenly Father, we come before you with humble hearts, seeking your guidance and wisdom as we embark on this journey of meditation and inner peace. Open our minds and hearts to the profound truths found within your Word, and grant us the grace to set aside the distractions of this world, that we may fully embrace the practice of meditating on your teachings. Help us to find strength, comfort, and peace in the promises of your unfailing love, and to draw ever closer to you through this sacred discipline. In Jesus' name, we pray. Amen.

The life of Jesus himself serves as a powerful example of the importance of meditation and finding solitude with God. Throughout the Gospels, we see Jesus frequently withdrawing to desolate places to pray and commune with the Father (Mark 1:35, Luke 5:16). These moments of quiet meditation allowed Him to renew His strength, seek divine guidance, and maintain an unwavering connection with God amidst the demands and pressures of His ministry.

Consider the story of Jesus' temptation in the wilderness (Matthew 4:1-11). After fasting for forty days and nights, Satan came to tempt Him, preying on His physical hunger and seeking to undermine His mission. But Jesus, grounded in the Word of God and the wisdom gained through meditation, was able to resist each temptation, countering the enemy's lies with the truth of Scripture. This powerful episode demonstrates the necessity of meditating on God's Word, allowing it to become a firm foundation upon which we can stand against the trials and temptations of this world.

In the New Testament, the apostle Paul also emphasizes the importance of meditation, encouraging believers to "think about the things that are good and worthy of praise" (Philippians 4:8 GNT). This exhortation reminds us that our thoughts have a profound impact on our emotions, our actions, and ultimately, our state of being. By consciously choosing to meditate on that which is pure, noble, and praiseworthy, we can cultivate an inner peace that transcends our circumstances.

Prayer:
Dear Lord, we come before you with open hearts, seeking to deepen our understanding of the sacred practice of meditation. Help us to follow the example of your Son, Jesus Christ, who often withdrew to spend time in prayer and communion with you. Grant us the wisdom and discipline to carve out moments of solitude, where we can quiet our minds and souls, and truly meditate on your Word and your presence in our lives. May these times of meditation strengthen our faith, renew our spirits, and draw us ever closer to you, the source of all peace and comfort. In Jesus' name, we pray. Amen.

Throughout the Bible, we find numerous examples of individuals who found solace, strength, and wisdom through the practice of meditation. Consider the story of Joshua, who was tasked with leading the Israelites into the Promised Land after the death of Moses. In the book of Joshua, we read, "This Book of the Law shall not depart from your mouth, but you shall meditate on it day and night, so that you may be careful to do according to all that is written in it" (Joshua 1:8 ESV). This command from God not only underscores the importance of meditating on His Word but also reveals the transformative power of such a practice – it enables us to walk in obedience to His will and to experience the blessings that come from aligning our lives with His purposes.

The life of King David also provides a poignant illustration of the role of meditation in cultivating inner peace and a deep relationship with God. In the Psalms, we catch glimpses of David's heart and his practice of meditating on the Lord's goodness, even in the midst of great adversity. In Psalm 63, he writes, "On my bed I remember you; I think of you through the watches of the night. Because you are my help, I sing in the shadow of your wings" (Psalm 63:6-7 NIV). Here, we see David finding comfort and peace in the remembrance of God's faithfulness, even in the darkness of night, through the practice of meditation.

As we journey through the Bible, we encounter countless other examples of individuals who found strength, wisdom, and inner peace through the discipline of meditation. From the prophet Habakkuk, who declared, "I will rejoice in the Lord, I will be joyful in God my Savior" (Habakkuk 3:18 NIV), to the apostle Paul, who exhorted believers to "pray without ceasing" (1 Thessalonians 5:17 ESV), the biblical foundation for meditation is woven throughout the very fabric of Scripture.

In essence, the practice of godly meditation is a means of aligning our hearts and minds with the heart and mind of God. It is a way of quieting the noise and distractions of this world, and instead, fixing our thoughts on the eternal truths and promises found in His Word. As we meditate on Scripture, we are transformed by the renewing of our minds (Romans 12:2), and we begin to experience the peace that surpasses all understanding (Philippians 4:7).

Moreover, meditation is not merely a solitary practice but also a means of cultivating a deeper sense of community and connection with fellow believers. As we meditate on God's Word together, we are united in our pursuit of His truth and our desire to walk in His ways. This shared experience of meditating on Scripture can foster a spirit of fellowship, accountability, and mutual encouragement, strengthening the bonds of our Christian community.

In a world that is constantly vying for our attention, the practice of godly

CHAPTER 1

meditation offers us a sacred refuge – a place where we can find rest for our souls, strength for the journey, and a profound sense of peace that can only come from an intimate relationship with our Heavenly Father. As we embrace this discipline and allow the truths of Scripture to permeate our hearts and minds, we will find ourselves transformed, our faith deepened, and our lives aligned with the purposes and plans of the One who loves us with an everlasting love.

CHAPTER 2

Preparing Your Mind and Heart for Meditation

"Be still, and know that I am God." - **Psalm 46:10 (NIV)**

In the midst of our fast-paced, modern lives, the act of being still can seem like an insurmountable challenge. Our minds are constantly bombarded with a barrage of stimuli, from the endless stream of notifications on our devices to the incessant demands of work, family, and social obligations. It is all too easy to become consumed by the noise and distractions of this world, leaving little room for the stillness and quiet reflection that are essential for a fruitful meditation practice.

And yet, it is in this very stillness that we find the pathway to true inner peace and a deeper connection with God. The Bible reminds us time and again of the importance of quieting our souls, of turning our focus away from the fleeting concerns of this world and fixing our gaze upon the eternal truths of our Heavenly Father.

In the book of Lamentations, the prophet Jeremiah offers this poignant exhortation: "Let us examine our ways and test them, and let us return to the Lord" (Lamentations 3:40 NIV). This verse underscores the necessity of introspection, of taking a step back from the busyness of life and honestly evaluating the state of our hearts and minds. It is through this process of self-examination that we can identify the areas in our lives that need to be surrendered to God, the thoughts and attitudes that are hindering our spiritual growth, and the distractions that are preventing us from experiencing the fullness of His peace.

Prayer:
Gracious God, we come before you with hearts that long for stillness and quietude. In a world that constantly clamors for our attention, we ask that you would grant us the wisdom and discipline to create sacred spaces of solitude, where we can turn our focus entirely toward you. Help us to let go of the distractions and worries that so often consume our thoughts, and instead, to embrace the stillness that allows us to truly know you as our Lord and Savior. May our minds and hearts be prepared for the transformative practice of meditation, that we might experience the depth of your peace and the richness of your presence. In Jesus' name, we pray. Amen.

The story of Mary and Martha, found in the Gospel of Luke, provides a powerful illustration of the importance of stilling our souls and prioritizing our time with the Lord. When Jesus visited their home, we are told that "Martha was distracted by all the preparations that had to be made" (Luke 10:40 NIV). In contrast, her sister Mary "sat at the Lord's feet listening to what he said" (Luke 10:39 NIV). When Martha expressed her frustration with Mary's apparent lack of concern for the household duties, Jesus gently rebuked her, saying, "Martha, Martha, you are worried and upset about many things, but few things are needed—or indeed only one. Mary has chosen what is better, and it will not be taken away from her" (Luke 10:41-42 NIV).

This story serves as a poignant reminder of the need to set aside the distractions and worries of this world, and instead, to prioritize our time with Jesus, sitting at His feet and allowing His words to penetrate our hearts and minds. It is in this posture of stillness and attentiveness that we can truly prepare ourselves for the practice of godly meditation, opening our souls to the transformative power of God's truth.

One of the key ways to cultivate this stillness and prepare our hearts for meditation is through the practice of silence. In our modern world, we are constantly surrounded by noise – the clamor of traffic, the chatter of television and radio, the endless notifications from our devices. While these sounds may seem innocuous, they can have a profound impact on our ability to quiet our minds and find inner peace.

The book of Ecclesiastes offers this wisdom: "There is a time for everything, and a season for every activity under the heavens... a time to be silent and a time to speak" (Ecclesiastes 3:1, 7 NIV). These words remind us of the importance of intentionally creating spaces of silence in our lives, moments where we can withdraw from the noise and distractions of the world and simply be present with God.

Consider the example of Jesus himself, who often retreated to desolate places to pray and commune with the Father (Luke 5:16). In these moments of solitude and silence, He found the strength and wisdom to carry out His ministry, to resist the temptations of the enemy, and to pour out His heart in intimate conversation with God.

As we seek to prepare our minds and hearts for the practice of godly meditation, we too must embrace the discipline of silence. This may involve setting aside specific times each day to unplug from our devices and external stimuli, finding a quiet place where we can simply be still and allow our thoughts to settle. It may also mean incorporating periods of silent reflection into our daily routines, perhaps before we start our day or as we wind down in the evening.

Prayer:
Heavenly Father, we come before you with hearts that long for the peace and stillness that can only be found in your presence. We confess that too often, we allow the noise and distractions of this world to consume our thoughts and steal our attention away from you. Forgive us for the times when we

have neglected the sacred practice of silence, and help us to embrace it as a means of preparing our souls for deeper communion with you. Grant us the discipline and determination to carve out moments of solitude, where we can turn off the constant barrage of external stimuli and simply rest in the assurance of your love and sovereignty. May these times of silence open our hearts and minds to the transformative power of your Word, and equip us for a more fruitful practice of meditation. In Jesus' name, we pray. Amen.

In addition to cultivating silence, another vital aspect of preparing our minds and hearts for meditation is the practice of confession and repentance. The Bible tells us that "if we claim to be without sin, we deceive ourselves and the truth is not in us" (1 John 1:8 NIV). As fallen human beings, we all carry the weight of sin and brokenness, which can create barriers in our relationship with God and hinder our ability to experience the fullness of His peace.

However, the good news is that through the sacrificial love of Jesus Christ, we have been offered the gift of forgiveness and the opportunity to have our hearts and minds cleansed from the stain of sin. The apostle John reminds us, "If we confess our sins, he is faithful and just and will forgive us our sins and purify us from all unrighteousness" (1 John 1:9 NIV).

As we approach the practice of godly meditation, it is essential that we take the time to examine our hearts and confess any areas of sin or brokenness that may be hindering our ability to connect with God on a deeper level. This act of confession and repentance is not merely a ritual, but rather a powerful tool for opening our hearts and minds to the transformative work of the Holy Spirit.

Consider the story of David, the psalmist and king of Israel. After committing the grievous sins of adultery and murder, David found himself weighed down by guilt and shame, his relationship with God fractured by his disobedience. It was only through a heartfelt act of confession and repentance, captured in Psalm 51, that David was able to experience the restoration of his soul and the renewal of his spirit. "Create in me a pure heart, O God, and renew a steadfast spirit within me," he cried out (Psalm 51:10 NIV).

As we seek to prepare our hearts and minds for the sacred practice of meditation, we too must be willing to engage in this process of confession and repentance. It may involve setting aside time for personal reflection, allowing the Holy Spirit to reveal areas of sin or brokenness that need to be brought into the light. It may also involve seeking accountability and support from fellow believers, as we strive to walk in obedience and cultivate a heart that is fully surrendered to God.

By taking the time to confess our sins and repent of any attitudes or behaviors that are hindering our relationship with God, we create space for His grace and forgiveness to flow into our lives. This act of humility and vulnerability not only prepares our hearts for a deeper experience of meditation but also opens the door to the peace and restoration that can only be found in the loving embrace of our Heavenly Father.

As we journey through this process of preparing our minds and hearts for meditation, it is important to remember that we are not called to do this work alone. The Bible assures us that "the Holy Spirit helps us in our weakness" (Romans 8:26 NIV), and that when we seek God with all our hearts, He will be found by us (Jeremiah 29:13).

So let us approach this discipline of preparation with humility and faith, trusting in the power of God's Spirit to guide us, to reveal the areas of our lives that need transformation, and to equip us with the stillness, silence, and purity of heart that will enable us to truly experience the depths of His peace through the practice of godly meditation.

CHAPTER 3

Meditating on God's Word

"Keep this Book of the Law always on your lips; meditate on it day and night, so that you may be careful to do everything written in it. Then you will be prosperous and successful."
- **Joshua 1:8 NIV**

At the very heart of the practice of godly meditation lies the Word of God – the living, breathing words that have been preserved for us in the pages of Scripture. From the earliest accounts of creation to the prophetic visions of the end times, the Bible is a wellspring of truth, wisdom, and revelation, offering us a glimpse into the heart and mind of our Heavenly Father.

It is within these sacred texts that we find the sustenance for our souls, the guidance for our lives, and the promises that anchor us in the midst of life's storms. As we meditate on God's Word, we are not merely engaging in a mental exercise or intellectual pursuit; rather, we are opening ourselves up to the transformative power of the Holy Spirit, allowing the truth of Scripture to penetrate the depths of our being and shape the very essence of who we are.

The practice of meditating on God's Word is not a novel concept; it is a discipline that has been woven into the fabric of the Christian faith since its earliest days. In the book of Psalms, we find numerous exhortations to meditate on the precepts and promises of God, such as "Blessed is the one... whose delight is in the law of the Lord, and who meditates on his law day and night" (Psalm 1:1-2 NIV).

Prayer:

Heavenly Father, we come before you with hearts that long to be immersed in the depths of your Word. We recognize that your Scriptures are not merely a collection of words, but rather a living and active revelation of your truth, your wisdom, and your love for us. As we embark on the sacred practice of meditating on your Word, we ask that you would open our minds and hearts to receive the transformative power of your truth. May the words of Scripture take root deep within us, shaping our thoughts, guiding our actions, and bringing us into a deeper understanding of who you are and the purposes you have for our lives. In Jesus' name, we pray. Amen.

One of the most powerful examples of meditating on God's Word can be found in the life of Jesus himself. Throughout the Gospels, we see the Son of God consistently turning to the Scriptures for guidance, wisdom, and strength. In the wilderness, when faced with the temptations of the enemy, Jesus countered each attack with the truth of Scripture, declaring, "It is written..." (Matthew 4:1-11).

This profound encounter serves as a potent reminder of the power and authority that lies within the Word of God. When we meditate on Scripture, filling our minds and hearts with its truth, we are equipping ourselves with the very sword of the Spirit (Ephesians 6:17), enabling us to stand firm against the assaults of the enemy and the temptations of this world.

Moreover, Jesus' life was a living embodiment of the Scriptures, as He fulfilled the prophecies and promises contained within the Old Testament. From His humble birth in Bethlehem to His sacrificial death on the cross, every aspect of His earthly ministry was a manifestation of the Word made flesh (John 1:14).

As we meditate on the accounts of His life, death, and resurrection, we are not only gaining a deeper understanding of the Scriptures but also encountering the very essence of God's love and redemptive plan for humanity.

The apostle Paul, in his letter to the Romans, underscores the transformative power of meditating on God's Word, stating, "Do not conform to the pattern of this world, but be transformed by the renewing of your mind. Then you will be able to test and approve what God's will is – his good, pleasing and perfect will" (Romans 12:2 NIV). Here, Paul highlights the connection between the renewal of our minds through the Word of God and our ability to discern and follow God's will for our lives.

As we meditate on Scripture, allowing its truths to take root within us, we are gradually transformed from the inside out. Our thoughts, beliefs, and perspectives are reshaped, aligning with the mind of Christ and enabling us to navigate the complexities of life with wisdom and discernment.

Consider the story of Mary, the mother of Jesus, who "treasured up all these things and pondered them in her heart" (Luke 2:19 NIV) after the shepherds had shared their encounter with the angelic hosts. In this moment, Mary exemplified the practice of meditating on the Word, pondering the significance of the events unfolding around her and allowing the promises of God to take root within her soul.

Prayer:
   Lord Jesus, we come before you in awe and reverence, recognizing that you are the living Word made flesh. As we meditate on the Scriptures, we are not merely studying words on a page, but rather encountering the very essence of who you are. Open our eyes to see the depth and richness of your truth as it is revealed in the pages of the Bible. Grant us the wisdom and discernment to understand the full context and meaning of your Word, and the humility to allow its teachings to transform our thoughts, attitudes, and actions. May our meditation on Scripture be a constant source of strength, comfort, and

guidance, equipping us to live lives that are pleasing and honoring to you. In your precious name, we pray. Amen.

As we delve into the practice of meditating on God's Word, it is important to recognize that this is not a passive endeavor; rather, it requires intentionality, discipline, and a willingness to engage with the Scriptures on a deeper level. One powerful method for achieving this is through the practice of lectio divina, a ancient approach to Scripture reading and meditation that has been embraced by believers throughout the centuries.

Lectio divina, which translates to "divine reading," involves four distinct phases: lectio (reading), meditatio (meditation), oratio (prayer), and contemplatio (contemplation). The process begins with a slow, intentional reading of a passage of Scripture, allowing the words to sink into our hearts and minds. This is followed by a period of meditation, where we ponder the meaning and implications of the text, considering how it speaks to our lives and circumstances.

As we meditate on the passage, we naturally transition into a time of prayer, pouring out our hearts to God and seeking His guidance and wisdom in applying the truths we have encountered. Finally, we enter into a state of contemplation, resting in the presence of God and allowing the depths of His Word to saturate our very being.

This practice of lectio divina invites us to slow down, to savor the richness of Scripture, and to engage with the Word of God in a multidimensional way. By reading, meditating, praying, and contemplating, we are allowing the truth of the Bible to penetrate the very core of our existence, shaping our thoughts, emotions, and actions in a profound and lasting way.

Another powerful tool for meditating on God's Word is the practice of memorization and recitation. Throughout the Scriptures, we are exhorted to "keep [God's] words in your heart and mind" (Proverbs 4:21 NIV) and to "bind them on your heart forever" (Proverbs 6:21 NIV). By committing key passages, verses, or even entire chapters to memory, we are embedding the truth of God's Word deep within our souls, making it readily available to us in times of need, temptation, or decision-making.

Consider the example of the psalmist, who declared, "I have hidden your word in my heart that I might not sin against you" (Psalm 119:11 NIV). By filling our minds and hearts with the Word of God, we are fortifying ourselves against the temptations and trials of this world, equipping ourselves with the wisdom and strength to navigate life's challenges with integrity and faithfulness.

As we meditate on God's Word through the practice of memorization and recitation, we are not only strengthening our spiritual foundation but also cultivating a deeper sense of intimacy with our Heavenly Father. The very act of speaking and meditating on His words has a way of drawing us closer to Him, of allowing His truth to permeate the depths of our being and transform us from the inside out.

Yet another powerful approach to meditating on Scripture is through the practice of journaling and reflection. By taking the time to write down our thoughts, insights, and questions as we engage with the Word of God, we are creating a record of our spiritual journey – a testament to the ways in which the truth of Scripture has spoken into our lives and shaped our understanding of who God is.

The act of journaling allows us to slow down, to ponder the depths of God's Word, and to wrestle with the implications of its teachings in a more deliberate and intentional way. It provides a space for us to process our thoughts, to record our prayers and supplications, and to trace the ways in which God has been faithful and present in our lives.

Moreover, the practice of journaling can serve as a powerful tool for accountability and growth. By revisiting our written reflections over time, we can observe the ways in which our understanding and application of Scripture have deepened and evolved, and we can identify areas where we may need to seek further guidance or pursue additional study.

As we embrace these various practices of meditating on God's Word – whether through lectio divina, memorization and recitation, or journaling and reflection – we are opening ourselves up to the transformative power of Scripture. We are allowing the truth of the Bible to take root within us, shaping our thoughts, our beliefs, and our very way of life.

In a world that is constantly clamoring for our attention and bombarding us with countless messages and distractions, the discipline of meditating on God's Word serves as an anchor for our souls, grounding us in the eternal truth and wisdom that can only be found in the pages of Scripture. As we make this practice a central part of our lives, we will find ourselves becoming more attuned to the voice of our Heavenly Father, more equipped to navigate the challenges and trials of this world, and more deeply rooted in the peace and assurance that can only come from an intimate relationship with the Living Word.

CHAPTER 4

Meditating through Prayer and Praise

"Rejoice always, pray continually, give thanks in all circumstances; for this is God's will for you in Christ Jesus." - **1 Thessalonians 5:16-18 NIV**

At the heart of the Christian faith lies the profound truth that we are called to a life of intimate communion with our Heavenly Father. Prayer is the sacred channel through which we can pour out our hearts, voice our deepest longings, and seek the guidance and wisdom of the One who knows us better than we know ourselves.

Yet, too often, our prayer lives can become ritualistic, reduced to a checklist of requests and supplications, devoid of the depth and intentionality that true communion with God requires. It is in these moments that the practice of meditating through prayer and praise can breathe new life into our spiritual journeys, transforming our times of prayer into sacred encounters with the Living God.

The Scriptures are replete with examples of men and women who understood the power and necessity of meditating through prayer and praise. Consider the psalmist, who declared, "I will meditate on your precepts and consider your ways" (Psalm 119:15 NIV). Here, we see a beautiful fusion of meditation, prayer, and the contemplation of God's truths, all woven together in a tapestry of spiritual devotion.

Prayer:

Heavenly Father, we come before you with hearts that long for a deeper, more meaningful prayer life. We recognize that true communion with you goes beyond mere words and rituals; it requires a posture of meditation, a willingness to dwell in your presence and allow your truth to permeate the depths of our souls. Teach us, Lord, to meditate through prayer and praise, to linger in the sacred spaces where we can encounter your love, your wisdom, and your transformative power. May our times of prayer become moments of profound intimacy with you, shaping our thoughts, our desires, and our very way of life. In the precious name of Jesus, we pray. Amen.

One of the most powerful examples of meditating through prayer can be found in the life of our Lord and Savior, Jesus Christ. Throughout the Gospels, we see Jesus retreating to quiet places, often rising before dawn, to spend time in prayer and communion with the Father (Mark 1:35, Luke 5:16). These moments of solitude and meditation were not mere formalities; they were the wellspring from which Jesus drew strength, wisdom, and the resolve to carry out His earthly mission.

Consider the account of Jesus' prayer in the Garden of Gethsemane, where He wrestled with the weight of the cross and the suffering that lay ahead (Matthew 26:36-46). In this sacred moment, we see Jesus pouring out His heart to the Father, expressing His anguish and surrendering His will to the divine plan of redemption. Yet, amidst the intensity of His prayer, we also catch glimpses of a deep, abiding trust in the Father's love and sovereignty – a trust that could only have been cultivated through a lifetime of meditating on the truths of Scripture and the promises of God.

As we seek to emulate the example of Christ in our own prayer lives, we too must embrace the practice of meditating through prayer and praise. This involves more than simply reciting a list of requests or uttering empty words; it requires a posture of humble surrender, a willingness to lay aside our agendas and to truly listen for the still, small voice of the Holy Spirit.

CHAPTER 4

One powerful way to cultivate this practice is through the discipline of silence and solitude. Just as Jesus often withdrew to desolate places to pray, we too must intentionally create spaces in our lives where we can escape the noise and distractions of this world and simply be present with our Heavenly Father.

In the book of Lamentations, we read, "Let us examine our ways and test them, and let us return to the Lord" (Lamentations 3:40 NIV). These words remind us of the importance of self-reflection, of taking the time to pause and consider the state of our hearts and our relationship with God. As we engage in this practice of silent meditation and self-examination, we open ourselves up to the convicting work of the Holy Spirit, allowing Him to reveal areas in our lives that need transformation or realignment with God's will.

Another powerful avenue for meditating through prayer and praise is the practice of worship and thanksgiving. The Scriptures are filled with exhortations to "sing to the Lord a new song" (Psalm 96:1 NIV) and to "enter his gates with thanksgiving and his courts with praise" (Psalm 100:4 NIV). When we engage in the act of worship, whether through song, dance, or the simple lifting of our voices in adoration, we are participating in a profound form of meditation – one that draws our focus away from the temporary concerns of this world and fixes our gaze upon the eternal majesty and glory of our Creator.

Consider the story of Mary, the sister of Martha, who chose to sit at the feet of Jesus and listen to His teachings (Luke 10:38-42). While her sister was distracted by the busyness of household tasks, Mary recognized the importance of meditating on the words of her Lord, of basking in His presence and allowing His truth to penetrate the depths of her soul. In this simple act of worship and attentiveness, Mary exemplified the heart of true meditation through prayer and praise.

Prayer:
  Lord Jesus, we come before you in humble adoration, recognizing that you

are the source of all wisdom, peace, and eternal life. We confess that too often, we have allowed the distractions and busyness of this world to separate us from the sacred practice of meditating through prayer and praise. Forgive us for the times when our prayer lives have become routine and devoid of the intentionality and depth that true communion with you requires. Teach us, Lord, to linger in your presence, to pour out our hearts before you in prayer, and to offer up the sacrifice of praise that is due your holy name. May our times of prayer and worship become moments of profound transformation, shaping our thoughts, our desires, and our very way of life. In the precious name of Jesus, we pray. Amen.

As we journey deeper into the practice of meditating through prayer and praise, it is vital that we recognize the power of praying and meditating on the Scriptures themselves. The Word of God is not merely a collection of ancient texts; it is a living, breathing revelation of the character, the promises, and the eternal truths of our Heavenly Father.

When we meditate on the passages of Scripture, allowing their words to sink deep into our hearts and minds, we are opening ourselves up to the transformative power of God's truth. We are inviting the Holy Spirit to illuminate our understanding, to reveal the depths of wisdom and insight contained within the pages of the Bible, and to shape our thoughts and perspectives according to the mind of Christ.

One powerful example of this can be found in the life of the apostle Paul, who often incorporated Scripture into his prayers and meditations. In his letter to the Ephesians, Paul writes, "I keep asking that the God of our Lord Jesus Christ, the glorious Father, may give you the Spirit of wisdom and revelation, so that you may know him better" (Ephesians 1:17 NIV). Here, we see Paul meditating on the truths of who God is – His glory, His wisdom, and His desire for us to know Him intimately – and weaving these truths into his prayers for the believers in Ephesus.

As we embrace the practice of meditating through prayer and praise, we too can draw upon the rich tapestry of Scripture, allowing its truths and promises to infuse our times of communion with God. We can pray the very words of the psalmists, echoing their cries of adoration and their pleas for divine guidance. We can meditate on the teachings of Jesus, allowing His parables and illustrations to shape our understanding of the Kingdom of God and our role as His followers.

Moreover, as we meditate on the Scriptures in prayer, we are not merely reciting words on a page; we are engaging in a sacred dialogue with the Living Word Himself. We are inviting the Author of Life to speak directly into our hearts and minds, to reveal the depths of His love and the magnitude of His redemptive plan for humanity.

In this way, the practice of meditating through prayer and praise becomes a profound act of worship, a sacred exchange between the Creator and His beloved creation. It is a holy moment in which we lay aside our own agendas and desires, and instead, align our hearts and minds with the eternal truths and purposes of our Heavenly Father.

As we journey through this life, we will inevitably face trials, challenges, and seasons of struggle. It is in these moments that the discipline of meditating through prayer and praise becomes an anchor for our souls, a source of strength and comfort that transcends our circumstances.

When we find ourselves overwhelmed by anxiety, fear, or doubt, we can turn to the Scriptures and meditate on the promises of God's unwavering love and faithfulness. We can pray the words of the psalmist, "When anxiety was great within me, your consolation brought me joy" (Psalm 94:19 NIV), allowing the truth of God's peace to wash over us and calm our troubled hearts.

In times of mourning or loss, we can meditate on the words of Jesus, who declared, "Blessed are those who mourn, for they will be comforted" (Matthew

5:4 NIV), finding solace in the assurance that our Heavenly Father is the God of all comfort, and that He will never leave us nor forsake us (Hebrews 13:5).

And in the face of temptation or spiritual warfare, we can meditate on the truth of Scripture and the power of the Holy Spirit, praying the words of the apostle Paul, "For our struggle is not against flesh and blood, but against the rulers, against the authorities, against the powers of this dark world and against the spiritual forces of evil in the heavenly realms" (Ephesians 6:12 NIV). In these moments, we can find strength and victory through the meditation of God's Word and the practice of prayer and praise.

Ultimately, the discipline of meditating through prayer and praise is not merely a spiritual exercise; it is a way of life, a constant posture of communion and intimacy with our Heavenly Father. As we embrace this sacred practice, we will find ourselves transformed from the inside out, our thoughts and desires increasingly aligned with the heart and mind of Christ.

And as we journey deeper into this life of prayer and praise, we will discover that we are not merely uttering words into the void; rather, we are participating in a divine conversation, a sacred exchange with the One who holds the universe in His hands and yet delights in the intimate fellowship of His children.

So let us resolve to cultivate the discipline of meditating through prayer and praise, allowing the truth of Scripture and the presence of the Holy Spirit to infuse our times of communion with God. For it is in these sacred moments that we will find the true source of inner peace, the wellspring of wisdom and strength that will sustain us through every season of life.

CHAPTER 5

Finding Peace in God's Presence

"You will keep in perfect peace those whose minds are steadfast, because they trust in you."
- Isaiah 26:3 NIV

In a world that is constantly in motion, filled with noise, distractions, and an endless barrage of demands on our time and attention, the concept of peace can seem elusive – a fleeting moment that slips through our fingers before we can fully grasp it. Yet, as followers of Christ, we are called to a life of peace that transcends our circumstances, a peace that can only be found in the unwavering presence of our Heavenly Father.

The Scriptures are replete with promises and exhortations concerning the peace that is ours in Christ Jesus. In the Gospel of John, we hear the tender words of our Savior: "Peace I leave with you; my peace I give you. I do not give to you as the world gives. Do not let your hearts be troubled and do not be afraid" (John 14:27 NIV). These words are not mere platitudes; they are a profound invitation to experience the deep, abiding peace that can only be found in the presence of the Prince of Peace Himself.

Prayer:
  Heavenly Father, we come before you with hearts that long for the peace that surpasses all understanding. In a world that is constantly in turmoil,

we seek refuge in your unwavering presence, the only true source of lasting tranquility and rest for our souls. Teach us, Lord, to fix our minds and hearts on you, to trust in your sovereign control over all things, and to find our peace in the assurance of your love and faithfulness. May we cultivate a lifestyle of abiding in your presence, allowing the peace of Christ to guard our hearts and minds against the anxieties and fears that so often assail us. In the precious name of Jesus, we pray. Amen.

One of the most profound examples of finding peace in God's presence can be found in the life of our Lord and Savior, Jesus Christ. Throughout the Gospels, we see Jesus retreating to desolate places, often rising before dawn, to spend time in prayer and communion with the Father (Mark 1:35, Luke 5:16). These moments of solitude and meditation were not mere formalities; they were the wellspring from which Jesus drew strength, wisdom, and the peace that sustained Him through the trials and challenges of His earthly ministry.

Consider the account of Jesus calming the storm, as recorded in the Gospel of Mark (Mark 4:35-41). In the midst of a raging tempest, with the waves crashing against the boat and the disciples gripped by fear, Jesus slept peacefully, His mind and heart anchored in the unwavering presence of the Father. When the disciples awakened Him, fraught with panic, Jesus simply spoke to the wind and the waves, commanding, "Peace, be still!" In an instant, the storm subsided, and a great calm settled over the sea.

This remarkable event serves as a powerful illustration of the peace that can be found in God's presence, even in the midst of life's most turbulent storms. When our minds and hearts are fixed on the Lord, trusting in His sovereign control over all things, we too can experience a supernatural calm that defies our circumstances and transcends the fears and anxieties that so often threaten to overwhelm us.

Throughout the Scriptures, we encounter numerous examples of individuals who found peace and refuge in the presence of God, even in the face of daunting challenges and adversities. Consider the story of David, the psalmist-king of Israel, who declared, "The Lord is my light and my salvation – whom shall I fear? The Lord is the stronghold of my life – of whom shall I be afraid?" (Psalm 27:1 NIV).

These words, penned during a time of great turmoil and upheaval in David's life, reveal the unwavering trust and confidence he placed in the Lord's presence and protection. Despite the threats and dangers that surrounded him, David found peace in the assurance that God was his stronghold, his refuge, and the source of his courage and strength.

In the book of Philippians, the apostle Paul echoes this sentiment, exhorting believers to "not be anxious about anything, but in every situation, by prayer and petition, with thanksgiving, present your requests to God. And the peace of God, which transcends all understanding, will guard your hearts and your minds in Christ Jesus" (Philippians 4:6-7 NIV). Here, Paul offers a powerful prescription for finding peace in the midst of life's storms: a life of prayer, thanksgiving, and a steadfast focus on the presence and promises of God.

Prayer:
Lord Jesus, we come before you in humble reverence, acknowledging that you are the Prince of Peace, the one in whom true and lasting tranquility can be found. We confess that too often, we have allowed the cares and concerns of this world to consume our thoughts and rob us of the peace that is ours in you. Forgive us for the times when we have neglected the sacred practice of abiding in your presence, for it is in your presence that our souls find rest and our hearts find refuge. Teach us, Lord, to cultivate a lifestyle of dwelling in your presence, of meditating on your truth, and of surrendering our anxieties and fears to your sovereign control. May we experience the fullness of the peace that transcends all understanding, a peace that guards our hearts and minds and empowers us to navigate the storms of life with unwavering faith and courage. In your precious name, we pray. Amen.

As we seek to find peace in God's presence, it is essential that we understand the inextricable link between peace and trust. The prophet Isaiah, in the verse that opened this chapter, highlights this connection: "You will keep in perfect peace those whose minds are steadfast, because they trust in you" (Isaiah 26:3 NIV). True peace, the kind that calms our souls and anchors us in the midst of life's storms, is predicated on our ability to trust in the Lord with unwavering faith.

This trust is not blind or naive; rather, it is rooted in a deep understanding of who God is – His character, His sovereignty, and His unfailing love for His children. When we meditate on the truths of Scripture and the promises of God, we cultivate a steadfast trust that enables us to surrender our fears, our anxieties, and our circumstances into His capable hands.

Consider the story of Abraham, the father of faith, who was called by God to leave the familiarity of his homeland and embark on a journey to an unknown land (Genesis 12:1-9). Despite the uncertainties and challenges that lay ahead, Abraham trusted in the Lord's promises and guidance, and his life became a testament to the peace that can be found in unwavering obedience and trust in God's plan.

As we journey through life, we will inevitably encounter situations that challenge our faith and tempt us to succumb to fear and anxiety. It is in these moments that the discipline of meditating on God's presence and trusting in His sovereign control becomes paramount. We can turn to the Scriptures and meditate on the words of the psalmist, who declared, "When I am afraid, I put my trust in you" (Psalm 56:3 NIV), finding solace and strength in the knowledge that our Heavenly Father is ever-present and ever-faithful.

Another vital aspect of finding peace in God's presence is the practice of surrender and letting go. Too often, we cling tightly to our own plans, our own desires, and our own understanding, failing to recognize that true peace can only be found when we surrender our lives fully to the Lord's will and purposes.

The apostle Paul offers a powerful exhortation in this regard, urging believers to "not conform to the pattern of this world, but be transformed by the renewing of your mind. Then you will be able to test and approve what God's will is – his good, pleasing and perfect will" (Romans 12:2 NIV). When we allow our minds to be renewed by the truth of God's Word and the guidance of the Holy Spirit, we are better equipped to discern and embrace the Lord's perfect will for our lives – a will that leads us into the depths of His peace and the fullness of His purposes.

Consider the example of Mary, the mother of Jesus, who responded to the angelic proclamation of her unique role in God's redemptive plan with these humble words: "I am the Lord's servant. May your word to me be fulfilled" (Luke 1:38 NIV). In this moment of surrender, Mary exemplified the essence of finding peace in God's presence – a willingness to let go of her own plans and desires and to embrace the Lord's will, even when it seemed incomprehensible or overwhelming.

As we cultivate a lifestyle of surrender and letting go, we open ourselves up to the peace that surpasses all understanding – a peace that transcends our circumstances and anchors our souls in the unwavering love and sovereignty of our Heavenly Father. It is in this posture of humble obedience and trust that we can truly experience the depths of God's presence and the fullness of His peace.

Yet, even as we strive to find peace in the presence of God, it is important to recognize that this journey is not without its challenges and struggles. The enemy of our souls will seek to disrupt our peace, to sow seeds of doubt and fear, and to distract us from the steadfast focus that is required to abide in the Lord's presence.

In these moments of spiritual warfare, it is essential that we turn to the truth of God's Word and the power of prayer, meditating on the promises of Scripture and seeking the guidance and strength of the Holy Spirit. We can take solace in the words of the apostle Paul, who reminds us that "the peace of God, which transcends all understanding, will guard your hearts and your minds in Christ Jesus" (Philippians 4:7 NIV).

As we meditate on these truths and cling to the promises of God's Word, we can find refuge and strength in the midst of life's storms, knowing that our Heavenly Father is ever-present, ever-faithful, and ever-committed to our well-being and eternal security in Christ.

Ultimately, the journey of finding peace in God's presence is not a destination to be reached, but rather a lifelong pursuit – a constant, intentional choice to fix our minds and hearts on the Lord, to trust in His sovereign control, and to surrender our lives fully to His perfect will and purposes.

As we embrace this sacred discipline, we will find ourselves transformed from the inside out, our thoughts and attitudes increasingly aligned with the mind of Christ and the peace that He offers to all who come to Him. And in the midst of life's trials and tribulations, we will experience a deep, abiding sense of tranquility – a peace that transcends our circumstances and anchors our souls in the unwavering love and faithfulness of our Heavenly Father.

So let us resolve to cultivate a lifestyle of dwelling in God's presence, meditating on His truth, and surrendering our lives to His perfect will. For it is in His presence that we will find the true and lasting peace that our souls so desperately crave – a peace that will sustain us through every season of life and ultimately lead us into the eternal rest and glory that awaits us in His heavenly kingdom.

CHAPTER 6

Overcoming Anxiety and Worry through Meditation

"Do not be anxious about anything, but in every situation, by prayer and petition, with thanksgiving, present your requests to God. And the peace of God, which transcends all understanding, will guard your hearts and your minds in Christ Jesus."
- Philippians 4:6-7 NIV

In a world that is constantly in motion, filled with uncertainties and challenges, it is all too easy to find ourselves consumed by anxiety and worry. Our minds race with a never-ending stream of "what ifs," and our hearts are gripped by fear and apprehension, robbing us of the peace and joy that are rightfully ours in Christ Jesus.

Yet, as followers of the Prince of Peace, we are called to a life that is marked by a profound sense of tranquility, a life where our thoughts and emotions are anchored in the unwavering promises of our Heavenly Father. It is in this truth that we find the antidote to anxiety and worry – the practice of godly meditation.

Prayer:
Heavenly Father, we come before you with hearts that are often weighed down by anxiety and worry. We confess that too frequently, we allow the cares and concerns of this world to consume our thoughts and rob us of the

peace that is ours in Christ Jesus. Forgive us for the times when we have failed to trust in your sovereign control and the assurance of your love and faithfulness. As we embark on this journey of overcoming anxiety and worry through meditation, we ask that you would renew our minds and transform our perspective. Teach us to fix our gaze upon you, the unchanging source of our strength and security. May our times of meditation be a refuge from the storms of life, a sacred space where we can find rest for our souls and a renewed sense of your perfect peace. In the precious name of Jesus, we pray. Amen.

The Scriptures are replete with examples of men and women who faced overwhelming circumstances and yet found solace and strength through the practice of godly meditation. Consider the story of David, the psalmist-king of Israel, who faced numerous threats and challenges throughout his life, from the pursuit of King Saul to the rebellion of his own son, Absalom. Yet, in the midst of these tumultuous circumstances, David found refuge in the presence of God and the practice of meditation.

In Psalm 55, we catch a glimpse of David's heart as he pours out his anxieties and fears before the Lord: "My heart is in anguish within me; the terrors of death have fallen on me. Fear and trembling have beset me; horror has overwhelmed me" (Psalm 55:4-5 NIV). These raw and honest words resonate with the depths of human emotion, echoing the struggles we all face when confronted with the uncertainties and trials of life.

Yet, even in the midst of his anguish, David turns to the practice of meditation, declaring, "But I call to God, and the Lord saves me. Evening, morning and noon I cry out in distress, and he hears my voice" (Psalm 55:16-17 NIV). Through the act of meditating on the character and promises of God, David finds the strength and courage to overcome his anxiety and worry, trusting in the Lord's unwavering love and faithfulness.

This powerful example serves as a reminder that even in the darkest moments of life, we can find solace and refuge through the practice of godly meditation. When our minds are consumed by fear and our hearts are gripped by worry, we can turn to the truth of God's Word and the discipline of prayer, allowing the peace of Christ to guard our hearts and minds (Philippians 4:7).

One of the most potent tools we have in the battle against anxiety and worry is the practice of meditating on the promises of Scripture. Throughout the Bible, we are reminded of God's unwavering commitment to care for His children, to provide for our needs, and to guard us from harm.

In the Sermon on the Mount, Jesus addresses the issue of anxiety head-on, exhorting His followers, "Therefore I tell you, do not worry about your life, what you will eat or drink; or about your body, what you will wear. Is not life more than food, and the body more than clothes?" (Matthew 6:25 NIV). He then goes on to remind us of the care and provision that our Heavenly Father extends to even the birds of the air and the flowers of the field, assuring us that we are far more valuable in His sight.

As we meditate on these words of truth, allowing them to penetrate the depths of our hearts and minds, we are reminded of the futility of anxiety and worry. We are called to place our trust in the One who holds the universe in His hands, the One who knows our every need and has promised to provide for us in His perfect timing and according to His perfect will.

Prayer:
Lord Jesus, we come before you with hearts that are often burdened by anxiety and worry. We confess that too often, we allow the cares and concerns of this world to consume our thoughts and rob us of the peace that is ours in you. Forgive us for the times when we have doubted your sovereign control and failed to trust in your unwavering love and provision. As we seek to overcome anxiety and worry through the practice of meditation, we ask that you would renew our minds and transform our perspective. Teach us to fix our gaze upon you, the unchanging source of our strength and security. May

our times of meditation be a refuge from the storms of life, a sacred space where we can find rest for our souls and a renewed sense of your perfect peace. In your precious name, we pray. Amen.

Another powerful weapon in our arsenal against anxiety and worry is the practice of meditating on the character and attributes of God Himself. When we fix our thoughts and meditations on who God is – His sovereignty, His love, His faithfulness, and His unwavering commitment to our well-being – we are reminded of the solid foundation upon which our faith rests.

In the book of Lamentations, the prophet Jeremiah offers a poignant example of this practice, declaring, "Yet this I call to mind and therefore I have hope: Because of the Lord's great love we are not consumed, for his compassions never fail. They are new every morning; great is your faithfulness" (Lamentations 3:21-23 NIV). Even in the midst of great sorrow and despair, Jeremiah found solace and hope by meditating on the character of God – His steadfast love, His unfailing compassion, and His unwavering faithfulness.

As we incorporate this practice into our own lives, meditating on the attributes of our Heavenly Father, we too can find strength and courage to face the anxieties and worries that threaten to overwhelm us. We can rest in the assurance that the God we serve is not a distant or indifferent deity, but rather a loving and compassionate Father who is intimately involved in every aspect of our lives.

The story of Jesus calming the storm, as recorded in the Gospel of Mark, provides a powerful illustration of the peace that can be found by meditating on the character and power of God (Mark 4:35-41). In the midst of a raging tempest, with the waves crashing against the boat and the disciples gripped by fear, Jesus slept peacefully, His mind and heart anchored in the unwavering presence and sovereignty of the Father.

CHAPTER 6

When the disciples awakened Him in a panic, Jesus simply spoke to the wind and the waves, commanding, "Peace, be still!" In an instant, the storm subsided, and a great calm settled over the sea. Through this miraculous display of power and authority, Jesus demonstrated the futility of anxiety and worry in the face of the One who holds dominion over the very forces of nature.

As we meditate on this account and countless others that reveal the power and sovereignty of our God, we are reminded that no circumstance, no challenge, and no storm is too great for the One who created the heavens and the earth. When our minds are fixed on the character and attributes of our Heavenly Father, we can find peace and refuge, even in the midst of life's most turbulent storms.

Yet another powerful tool in our quest to overcome anxiety and worry through meditation is the practice of thanksgiving and praise. The Scriptures are filled with exhortations to "give thanks in all circumstances" (1 Thessalonians 5:18 NIV) and to "enter his gates with thanksgiving and his courts with praise" (Psalm 100:4 NIV).

When we intentionally shift our focus from the anxieties and worries that threaten to consume us, and instead meditate on the countless blessings and provisions of our Heavenly Father, our perspective is transformed. We are reminded of the goodness and faithfulness of God, and our hearts are filled with gratitude, supplanting the fear and apprehension that once held sway.

Consider the example of the apostle Paul, who wrote from a Roman prison cell, "Rejoice in the Lord always. I will say it again: Rejoice!" (Philippians 4:4 NIV). Despite his circumstances, which could have easily fueled anxiety and worry, Paul chose to meditate on the joy and peace that could only be found in his relationship with Christ. His perspective was one of thanksgiving and praise, even in the midst of trials and hardships.

As we cultivate this practice of thanksgiving and praise in our own lives, meditating on the goodness and faithfulness of God, we too can experience a profound sense of peace and tranquility, even in the face of adversity. Our anxieties and worries are put into proper perspective, and our hearts are filled with a deep gratitude for the One who holds our lives in His capable hands.

Ultimately, the path to overcoming anxiety and worry through meditation is a journey that requires intentionality, discipline, and a willingness to surrender our fears and concerns to the Lord. It is a process of renewing our minds and transforming our perspectives, allowing the truth of God's Word and the power of His presence to permeate every aspect of our lives.

As we embrace this sacred discipline, we will find ourselves increasingly attuned to the voice of the Holy Spirit, who guides us into all truth and comforts us in our times of distress. We will experience the fullness of the peace that surpasses all understanding, a peace that guards our hearts and minds and anchors us in the unwavering love and faithfulness of our Heavenly Father.

So let us resolve to make the practice of godly meditation a central part of our lives, a daily discipline that equips us to overcome anxiety and worry. Let us meditate on the promises of Scripture, the character and attributes of God, and the countless reasons we have to offer thanksgiving and praise. For it is in these sacred moments of meditation that we will find the true and lasting peace that our souls so desperately crave – a peace that will sustain us through every season of life and ultimately lead us into the eternal rest and glory that awaits us in the presence of our Lord and Savior, Jesus Christ.

CHAPTER 7

Meditating on God's Creation and Nature

"The heavens declare the glory of God; the skies proclaim the work of his hands. Day after day they pour forth speech; night after night they reveal knowledge." -
Psalm 19:1-2 NIV

From the majestic peaks of towering mountains to the intricate beauty of a single flower, the wonders of God's creation surround us, offering a breathtaking testimony to the power, wisdom, and artistry of our Heavenly Father. As we take the time to observe and meditate on the marvels of nature, we are invited to step beyond the confines of our own limited understanding and catch a glimpse of the boundless majesty of the One who spoke the universe into existence.

In the busyness of our modern lives, it is all too easy to become disconnected from the natural world, to overlook the divine handiwork that surrounds us and lose sight of the profound truths that it reveals. Yet, the Scriptures offer a resounding call to open our eyes and our hearts to the majesty of God's creation, using it as a catalyst for deeper meditation, worship, and spiritual renewal.

Prayer:
   Heavenly Father, we come before you with hearts in awe of the wonders of your creation. From the vast expanses of the cosmos to the intricate details

of the smallest creature, your handiwork is on display, revealing your infinite power, wisdom, and creativity. As we embark on this journey of meditating on the marvels of nature, we ask that you would open our eyes to the profound truths and lessons that your creation has to teach us. May our times spent in the beauty of your natural world draw us closer to you, deepening our appreciation for your majesty and leading us into a deeper sense of worship and reverence. In the precious name of Jesus, we pray. Amen.

The book of Genesis offers a powerful account of the creation of the world, painting a vivid picture of the Lord's sovereign hand in crafting the heavens and the earth, the seas and the land, and every living creature that inhabits them. As we meditate on these verses, we are reminded of the sheer magnitude and complexity of God's creative work, a testament to His boundless wisdom and power.

Consider the words of the psalmist, who declares, "By the word of the Lord the heavens were made, their starry host by the breath of his mouth" (Psalm 33:6 NIV). This poetic description invites us to ponder the vastness of the universe, the countless galaxies and stars that stretch across the heavens, all brought into existence by the mere breath of our Creator.

As we gaze upon the night sky, allowing the majesty of the cosmos to fill our vision, we are reminded of the infinite greatness of our God and the insignificance of our own finite existence. Yet, in this humbling realization, we find a profound sense of awe and wonder, a reminder that the same God who spoke the universe into being has chosen to reveal Himself to us and invite us into a personal relationship with Him.

The apostle Paul echoes this sentiment in his letter to the Romans, declaring, "For since the creation of the world God's invisible qualities – his eternal power and divine nature – have been clearly seen, being understood from what has been made, so that people are without excuse" (Romans 1:20 NIV). Through the intricate design and beauty of the natural world, God has provided a clear and unmistakable revelation of His existence, His power, and His divine nature, leaving humanity without excuse for failing to recognize and worship Him as the Creator.

As we meditate on the wonders of God's creation, we are not only invited to marvel at the beauty and complexity of the natural world but also to contemplate the deeper spiritual truths that it reveals. The changing seasons, the cycle of life and death, and the delicate balance of ecosystems all point to the wisdom and sovereignty of our Heavenly Father, who orchestrates the intricate dance of nature with precision and purpose.

Prayer:

Lord Jesus, we stand in awe of your handiwork, displayed in the breathtaking beauty and complexity of your creation. From the towering mountains to the vast expanse of the oceans, from the delicate beauty of a single flower to the intricate design of the smallest creature, your artistry and wisdom are on full display. As we meditate on the wonders of nature, we are reminded of your infinite greatness and the depth of your love for us, your cherished creation. May our times spent in the beauty of your natural world draw us ever closer to you, deepening our appreciation for your majesty and leading us into a deeper sense of worship and reverence. In your precious name, we pray. Amen.

One of the most profound examples of meditating on God's creation can be found in the life of our Lord and Savior, Jesus Christ. Throughout the Gospels, we see Jesus frequently withdrawing to desolate places, often to pray and commune with the Father in the solitude of nature (Mark 1:35, Luke 5:16). These moments of solitude and meditation allowed Him to renew His strength, seek divine guidance, and maintain an unwavering connection with God amidst the demands and pressures of His ministry.

Consider the account of Jesus' transfiguration, as recorded in the Gospel of Matthew (Matthew 17:1-8). In this remarkable event, Jesus takes Peter,

James, and John up to a high mountain, where His appearance is transformed, and His divine glory is revealed. It is in this sacred, natural setting that the disciples catch a glimpse of the Lord's true nature and receive a profound revelation of His identity as the Son of God.

This powerful story reminds us that the beauty and majesty of the natural world can serve as a backdrop for profound spiritual encounters and revelations. As we meditate on the wonders of God's creation, we too can experience a deeper sense of His presence and a greater understanding of His character and purposes.

Another example of meditating on God's creation can be found in the life of the prophet Elijah. After a powerful confrontation with the prophets of Baal, Elijah flees into the wilderness, where he encounters the Lord in a powerful and unexpected way. As recorded in 1 Kings 19, the Lord passed by Elijah, manifesting His presence not in the powerful wind, earthquake, or fire, but in a gentle whisper (1 Kings 19:11-13).

This remarkable encounter reminds us that the Lord often speaks to us in the stillness and quietude of nature, inviting us to slow down, to listen, and to meditate on His voice amidst the beauty and tranquility of His creation. As we intentionally seek out these sacred spaces, we open ourselves up to the possibility of profound spiritual encounters and a deeper revelation of God's character and purposes.

Furthermore, the practice of meditating on God's creation is not merely an individual endeavor; it can also be a powerful tool for cultivating a sense of community and shared worship. Throughout the Scriptures, we see examples of God's people gathering together to celebrate and give thanks for the wonders of the natural world.

In the book of Leviticus, the Lord instructs the Israelites to observe various festivals and celebrations, many of which were tied to the rhythms and cycles of the agricultural calendar (Leviticus 23). These gatherings not only fostered a sense of community and unity among God's people but also served as opportunities to meditate on the Lord's provision and sovereignty, as evidenced in the fruitfulness of the land and the changing of the seasons.

As we come together as believers to marvel at the beauty of God's creation, whether through organized events or spontaneous moments of shared appreciation, we are reminded of the common bond we share as members of the same spiritual family. Our individual experiences of meditating on the natural world are woven together into a tapestry of worship and reverence, drawing us closer to one another and to the One who created us all.

Moreover, the practice of meditating on God's creation can serve as a powerful tool for evangelism and outreach. The wonders of the natural world are a universal language, transcending cultural and linguistic barriers, and offering a compelling testimony to the existence and power of our Creator.

As we share our experiences of meditating on the marvels of nature with those around us, we have the opportunity to point them to the ultimate source of beauty, order, and design – our Heavenly Father. We can echo the words of the psalmist, who declared, "The heavens declare the glory of God; the skies proclaim the work of his hands" (Psalm 19:1 NIV), inviting others to join us in worshiping and marveling at the One who created the cosmos.

Ultimately, the practice of meditating on God's creation is a journey that invites us to step beyond the confines of our own limited understanding and catch a glimpse of the boundless majesty of our Creator. It is a call to slow down, to observe, and to allow the beauty and complexity of the natural world to fill our hearts and minds with a sense of awe and wonder.

As we embrace this sacred discipline, we will find ourselves drawn ever closer to the One who spoke the universe into existence, our hearts overflowing with gratitude and praise for the majesty of His handiwork. We will discover that the wonders of creation are not merely beautiful scenery or scientific curiosities but rather a living testament to the power, wisdom, and artistry of our Heavenly Father.

So let us resolve to cultivate the practice of meditating on God's creation, whether it be through intentional moments of solitude in nature, shared experiences of appreciation and worship, or through the intentional exploration and study of the marvels that surround us. For it is in these sacred moments that we will find our souls refreshed, our spirits renewed, and our hearts aligned with the heart of the Creator Himself, who invites us to marvel at the wonders of His handiwork and to find true and lasting peace in His presence.

CHAPTER 8

Incorporating Meditation into Your Daily Routine

"But his delight is in the law of the Lord, and on his law he meditates day and night."
- Psalm 1:2 NIV

In a world that is constantly in motion, filled with a never-ending barrage of demands, distractions, and responsibilities, the practice of godly meditation can often feel like a luxury reserved for those with ample time and resources. Yet, the truth is that the discipline of meditation is not meant to be a fleeting or occasional endeavor; rather, it is a way of life, a constant posture of intentionality that permeates every aspect of our daily routines.

The Scriptures are replete with exhortations to make the practice of meditation a central part of our lives, a daily discipline that shapes our thoughts, our actions, and our very way of being. In the opening verses of the book of Psalms, we are introduced to the concept of the "blessed" individual, one whose "delight is in the law of the Lord, and on his law he meditates day and night" (Psalm 1:1-2 NIV).

Prayer:
Heavenly Father, we come before you with hearts that long to make the practice of godly meditation a constant and integral part of our daily lives. We

confess that too often, we allow the busyness and distractions of this world to crowd out the sacred spaces of stillness and reflection that are essential for cultivating a life of true peace and intimacy with you. Teach us, Lord, to prioritize and intentionally carve out moments throughout our days for the discipline of meditation, that we might find ourselves increasingly attuned to your voice and your truth. May our daily routines be infused with a spirit of reverence and worship, as we make the conscious choice to fix our thoughts on you and the eternal truths revealed in your Word. In the precious name of Jesus, we pray. Amen.

One of the most profound examples of incorporating meditation into daily life can be found in the life of our Lord and Savior, Jesus Christ. Throughout the Gospels, we see Jesus consistently setting aside time to retreat from the demands of His ministry, often rising before dawn or lingering late into the night to spend precious moments in prayer and communion with the Father (Mark 1:35, Luke 6:12).

These moments of intentional meditation and solitude were not mere formalities for Jesus; they were the very heartbeat of His life and ministry, the wellspring from which He drew strength, wisdom, and the unwavering focus that enabled Him to carry out the Father's will with such profound impact and authority.

Consider the account of Jesus' temptation in the wilderness, as recorded in the Gospel of Matthew (Matthew 4:1-11). After fasting for forty days and nights, Jesus was confronted by the enemy, who sought to undermine His mission and challenge His identity as the Son of God. Yet, in the face of these temptations, Jesus remained steadfast, countering each assault with the truth of Scripture – truth that He had undoubtedly meditated upon and internalized throughout His daily routines.

This powerful example serves as a reminder that incorporating the practice of meditation into our daily lives is not merely a matter of convenience or personal preference; it is a matter of spiritual survival. When we intentionally set aside time each day to meditate on God's Word, to commune with the Father in prayer, and to align our thoughts and desires with the truth of Scripture, we are fortifying ourselves against the attacks of the enemy and equipping ourselves with the strength and wisdom to navigate the challenges and temptations that will inevitably come our way.

In the book of Deuteronomy, the Lord instructs His people to "impress [His words] on your children. Talk about them when you sit at home and when you walk along the road, when you lie down and when you get up" (Deuteronomy 6:7 NIV). This exhortation highlights the importance of integrating the practice of meditation into the fabric of our daily routines, making it a natural and seamless part of our lives, woven into the very rhythms of our waking and sleeping hours.

Prayer:
   Lord Jesus, we come before you with a deep longing to make the practice of godly meditation a consistent and integral part of our daily lives. We confess that too often, we have allowed the busyness and distractions of this world to crowd out the sacred spaces of stillness and reflection that are essential for cultivating a life of true peace and intimacy with you. Forgive us for the times when we have neglected this vital discipline, and renew within us a sense of urgency and intentionality when it comes to incorporating meditation into our daily routines. Teach us, Lord, to prioritize and carve out moments throughout our days for the purpose of fixing our thoughts on you and the eternal truths revealed in your Word. May our daily activities be infused with a spirit of reverence and worship, as we make the conscious choice to align our hearts and minds with your heart and your purposes. In your precious name, we pray. Amen.

One practical way to incorporate meditation into our daily routines is to establish set times dedicated specifically to this sacred practice. For some, this may mean rising early in the morning before the demands of the day begin, finding solitude and stillness in the quiet hours before dawn. For others, it may involve carving out moments of reflection during the workday, perhaps during a lunch break or a brief pause between meetings or appointments.

The Scriptures offer numerous examples of individuals who made the practice of meditation a consistent part of their daily lives, regardless of their circumstances or responsibilities. The prophet Daniel, even while serving in the court of a pagan king, maintained his commitment to prayer and meditation, setting aside time each day to commune with the Lord (Daniel 6:10).

As we seek to establish these set times for meditation within our own daily routines, it is important to approach this discipline with intentionality and reverence. This may involve creating a dedicated space within our homes or workplaces – a quiet corner, a peaceful garden, or even a simple chair – where we can retreat from the distractions of the world and focus our thoughts and hearts on the Lord.

Additionally, we can incorporate various aids and tools to enhance our times of meditation, such as devotional readings, worship music, or even the practice of journaling, which can help us to process our thoughts and reflections in a more meaningful way.

Yet, while establishing set times for meditation is undoubtedly important, the practice of godly meditation should not be confined solely to these designated moments. Rather, it should permeate every aspect of our daily lives, infusing our thoughts and actions with a spirit of worship and reverence.

In the book of Colossians, the apostle Paul exhorts believers to "let the word of Christ dwell in you richly as you teach and admonish one another with all wisdom through psalms, hymns, and songs from the Spirit, singing to God with gratitude in your hearts" (Colossians 3:16 NIV). This verse highlights the importance of allowing the truth of Scripture to saturate our very beings, to shape our interactions and relationships, and to infuse our daily routines with a spirit of gratitude and worship.

As we intentionally set our minds on the things of God throughout the day – whether it be through the recitation of Scripture, the singing of praises, or the simple act of offering up prayers of gratitude – we are cultivating a lifestyle of meditation, a constant posture of attentiveness to the voice and presence of our Heavenly Father.

Consider the example of the apostle Paul himself, who, even in the midst of his extensive travels and trials, maintained a steadfast commitment to the practice of meditation. In his letter to the Philippians, he encourages believers to "rejoice in the Lord always" (Philippians 4:4 NIV), a exhortation that reflects his own daily choice to fix his thoughts and meditations on the goodness and faithfulness of God, regardless of his circumstances.

As we incorporate the practice of godly meditation into our daily routines, we too can experience the transformative power of this discipline, finding ourselves increasingly attuned to the voice of the Holy Spirit and the eternal truths of Scripture. Our thoughts, our words, and our actions will begin to reflect the mind of Christ, and we will find ourselves navigating the challenges and demands of life with a profound sense of peace and purpose.

However, it is important to recognize that the journey of incorporating meditation into our daily lives is not without its challenges and obstacles. The enemy of our souls will seek to distract us, to sow seeds of doubt and discouragement, and to lure us away from the sacred discipline of meditation with the promises of temporary pleasures or fleeting distractions.

In these moments of struggle and temptation, it is essential that we turn to the truth of God's Word and the power of prayer, seeking the strength and guidance of the Holy Spirit to persevere in the practice of godly meditation. We can find comfort and encouragement in the words of the psalmist, who declared, "I rise before dawn and cry for help; I have put my hope in your word" (Psalm 119:147 NIV).

As we journey through the process of incorporating meditation into our daily routines, we must also be willing to extend grace to ourselves and one another. There will be days when our times of meditation feel dry or unfulfilling, when our minds wander, and our focus is pulled in a thousand different directions. In these moments, we can cling to the truth that our Heavenly Father is not concerned with the perfection of our practice, but rather with the posture of our hearts and our willingness to seek Him consistently, day by day.

Ultimately, the discipline of incorporating meditation into our daily routines is not a destination to be reached, but rather a lifelong journey – a constant choice to align our thoughts, our words, and our actions with the truth of God's Word and the guidance of the Holy Spirit. As we embrace this sacred practice, we will find ourselves transformed from the inside out, our lives increasingly reflecting the peace, joy, and purpose that can only be found in an intimate relationship with our Lord and Savior, Jesus Christ.

So let us resolve to make the practice of godly meditation a central and integral part of our daily lives, weaving it into the very fabric of our routines and activities. May our mornings be filled with the stillness and solitude of intentional meditation, our middays infused with moments of gratitude and worship, and our evenings punctuated by the recitation of Scripture and the offering of prayers. For it is in these sacred moments, woven throughout the tapestry of our daily lives, that we will find true and lasting peace – a peace that transcends our circumstances and anchors our souls in the unwavering love and faithfulness of our Heavenly Father.

CHAPTER 9

The Role of Community and Fellowship in Meditation

"And let us consider how we may spur one another on toward love and good deeds, not giving up meeting together, as some are in the habit of doing, but encouraging one another—and all the more as you see the Day approaching." - **Hebrews 10:24-25 NIV**

In our modern world, which often celebrates individualism and self-reliance, it can be tempting to view the practice of godly meditation as a solitary endeavor – a personal journey of self-discovery and spiritual growth that is best undertaken in isolation. Yet, the truth is that the Christian faith has always been rooted in the concept of community, a shared experience of walking together in the light of God's truth and the fellowship of His love.

The Scriptures offer a resounding affirmation of the vital role that community and fellowship play in our spiritual lives, and the practice of meditation is no exception. From the earliest days of the Church, believers have gathered together to encourage one another, to share in the study of God's Word, and to cultivate a collective posture of worship and reverence.

Prayer:
Heavenly Father, we come before you with grateful hearts, acknowledging the gift of community and fellowship that you have bestowed upon us as your children. We recognize that the journey of faith is not meant to be walked

alone, but rather in the company of fellow believers who can encourage us, challenge us, and spur us on toward a deeper love and understanding of you. As we explore the role of community in the practice of godly meditation, we ask that you would open our eyes to the profound blessings and opportunities that arise when we gather together in your name. May our times of fellowship and shared meditation serve to strengthen our bonds of unity, deepen our appreciation for your truth, and ultimately draw us closer to you and to one another. In the precious name of Jesus, we pray. Amen.

One of the most powerful examples of the role of community in meditation can be found in the very beginnings of the Church, as recorded in the book of Acts. In the days following the outpouring of the Holy Spirit on the Day of Pentecost, we read that "they devoted themselves to the apostles' teaching and to fellowship, to the breaking of bread and to prayer" (Acts 2:42 NIV).

This early community of believers understood the importance of gathering together not only for instruction and the study of God's Word but also for the purpose of shared prayer and meditation. They recognized that the practice of collective worship and reflection had the power to strengthen their faith, deepen their understanding of the truth, and foster a sense of unity and belonging.

Throughout the New Testament epistles, we find numerous exhortations and encouragements related to the importance of community and fellowship in our spiritual lives. The apostle Paul, writing to the church in Colossae, urged them to "let the message of Christ dwell among you richly as you teach and admonish one another with all wisdom through psalms, hymns, and songs from the Spirit, singing to God with gratitude in your hearts" (Colossians 3:16 NIV).

These words highlight the transformative power of shared worship, meditation, and the study of God's Word within the context of community. When we gather together to sing praises, recite Scripture, and collectively reflect on the truths of the gospel, we are not only strengthening our individual walks with the Lord but also cultivating a shared experience of reverence and adoration.

Consider the example of the early Church fathers, who recognized the importance of communal meditation and established the practice of lectio divina, a structured approach to Scripture reading and reflection that was often undertaken in small groups or monastic communities. Through the collective engagement with God's Word, these believers sought to deepen their understanding of the truth and to foster a spirit of unity and accountability.

Prayer:
Lord Jesus, we come before you with hearts that long for the richness of community and fellowship that can only be found in your presence. We recognize that the journey of meditation and spiritual growth is not one that we were meant to walk alone, but rather in the company of fellow believers who can encourage us, challenge us, and spur us on toward a deeper love and understanding of you. As we gather together in your name, we ask that you would pour out your Spirit upon us, cultivating an atmosphere of unity, trust, and vulnerability. May our times of shared meditation and reflection serve to strengthen the bonds of our community, deepen our appreciation for your truth, and ultimately draw us closer to you and to one another. In your precious name, we pray. Amen.

The benefits of embracing the practice of meditation within the context of community are manifold. When we gather together with fellow believers for the purpose of shared worship, prayer, and the study of Scripture, we create a sacred space where we can encourage one another, hold each other accountable, and collectively seek the guidance and wisdom of the Holy Spirit.

In the book of Proverbs, we are reminded that "as iron sharpens iron, so one person sharpens another" (Proverbs 27:17 NIV). This metaphor speaks to the power of community and the transformative impact that we can have on one another when we come together in a spirit of mutual support and accountability.

As we share our personal experiences, insights, and struggles related to the practice of meditation, we create an environment where we can learn from one another, challenge one another's perspectives, and offer encouragement and wisdom gleaned from our collective journeys with the Lord.

Moreover, the practice of communal meditation can serve as a powerful antidote to the isolation and loneliness that can often accompany our spiritual walks. In a world that increasingly celebrates individualism and self-reliance, the act of gathering together with fellow believers for the purpose of shared worship and reflection can provide a sense of belonging and connection that is essential for our spiritual well-being.

The story of the early Church, as recorded in the book of Acts, provides a compelling example of the transformative power of community and fellowship. In the aftermath of the outpouring of the Holy Spirit on the Day of Pentecost, we read that "all the believers were together and had everything in common" (Acts 2:44 NIV). This shared experience of fellowship and unity not only strengthened the bonds of their community but also empowered them to boldly proclaim the gospel and to live as witnesses to the truth of Christ's resurrection.

As we seek to cultivate a similar spirit of community and fellowship in our own spiritual lives, we can look to the example of the early Church and embrace practices such as shared meals, corporate prayer, and the collective study and meditation of God's Word. These activities not only foster a sense of belonging and unity but also create opportunities for deep spiritual growth and transformation.

Yet, it is important to recognize that the practice of communal meditation is not without its challenges. In a world that often prioritizes efficiency and productivity, the idea of setting aside dedicated time for collective worship and reflection can seem impractical or even indulgent. Additionally, the act of sharing our personal struggles and insights with others can feel intimidating or uncomfortable, particularly in a culture that often celebrates self-reliance and individualism.

However, it is in these moments of vulnerability and shared experience that we can find the true depth and richness of community. When we are willing to open our hearts and minds to one another, to share our struggles and triumphs, and to collectively seek the guidance and wisdom of the Holy Spirit, we create a sacred space where true transformation can take place.

The story of the disciples on the road to Emmaus, as recorded in the Gospel of Luke, provides a powerful illustration of the role of community and fellowship in the practice of meditation (Luke 24:13-35). After encountering the risen Christ, these two disciples return to Jerusalem and share their experience with the other disciples. As they gather together and recount the events of that day, the risen Lord himself appears in their midst, opening their eyes to the truth of Scripture and kindling within them a renewed sense of hope and purpose.

This profound encounter serves as a reminder that when we come together as a community of believers, offering our collective experiences and insights, we create an environment where the Lord can move in powerful and unexpected ways. Our shared meditations and reflections become a catalyst for divine revelation and a deeper understanding of the truth.

As we embrace the practice of communal meditation and fellowship, we must also be willing to extend grace and understanding to one another. Just as our individual journeys with the Lord are marked by seasons of growth and struggle, so too will our experiences of shared worship and reflection ebb and flow.

There may be times when our gatherings feel dry or lacking in spiritual vitality, when the flames of our collective passion seem to wane. In these moments, it is essential that we remain steadfast in our commitment to one another, offering encouragement and support, and trusting in the Lord's faithfulness to renew our spirits and reignite the fires of our devotion.

Ultimately, the role of community and fellowship in the practice of godly meditation is not merely a suggestion or a optional component of our spiritual lives; it is a vital and essential aspect of our journey with the Lord. When we gather together with fellow believers for the purpose of shared worship, prayer, and the study of God's Word, we are participating in a sacred tradition that has been woven into the fabric of the Christian faith since its earliest days.

As we embrace this practice of communal meditation, we will find ourselves increasingly attuned to the voice of the Holy Spirit, our understanding of the truth deepened, and our bonds of fellowship strengthened. We will experience the transformative power of collective worship and reverence, and we will be emboldened to live as witnesses to the truth of the gospel, proclaiming the love and salvation of our Lord and Savior, Jesus Christ.

So let us resolve to make the practice of communal meditation a central part of our spiritual journeys, seeking out opportunities to gather with fellow believers for the purpose of shared worship, prayer, and the study of God's Word. May our times of fellowship and collective reflection serve as sacred spaces where we can encourage one another, hold each other accountable, and collectively seek the guidance and wisdom of the Holy Spirit. For it is in these moments of shared experience and unity that we will find the true depth and richness of the Christian life, and the peace that can only be found in the presence of our Heavenly Father and the community of His beloved children.

CHAPTER 10

Sharing the Peace of Christ with Others

"Blessed are the peacemakers, for they will be called children of God."
- Matthew 5:9 NIV

As followers of Christ, we are called to be ambassadors of peace – not merely for our own personal benefit, but for the sake of a world that is desperately in need of the hope and reconciliation that can only be found in the gospel. The practice of godly meditation is not merely a means of cultivating inner tranquility; it is a transformative journey that equips us to be agents of change, radiating the peace of Christ into every sphere of our lives and every relationship we encounter.

The Scriptures offer a resounding affirmation of our calling to be peacemakers, to embrace the ministry of reconciliation, and to share the good news of God's redemptive love with a hurting and broken world. As we journey deeper into the practice of meditation, we are not only transformed from the inside out, but we are also empowered to be vessels of the Lord's peace, carrying His message of hope and healing to those around us.

Prayer:
Heavenly Father, we come before you with hearts that long to be ambassadors of your peace in a world that is often consumed by conflict, fear, and brokenness. We recognize that the practice of godly meditation is not merely

a means of personal growth and transformation, but also a sacred calling to share the hope and reconciliation of the gospel with those around us. As we explore what it means to be peacemakers and bearers of your truth, we ask that you would open our eyes to the opportunities that surround us, and fill our hearts with a deep sense of compassion and love for those who have yet to experience the fullness of your peace. May our lives be a testament to the transformative power of your love, and may our words and actions serve as beacons of hope, drawing others into the embrace of your eternal peace. In the precious name of Jesus, we pray. Amen.

One of the most powerful examples of sharing the peace of Christ can be found in the life and ministry of our Lord and Savior, Jesus Christ. Throughout the Gospels, we see Jesus consistently reaching out to those who were marginalized, oppressed, and forgotten by society – offering them not only physical healing but also the hope and peace that can only be found in the embrace of God's love.

Consider the account of the woman at the well, as recorded in the Gospel of John (John 4:1-42). In this remarkable encounter, Jesus initiates a conversation with a Samaritan woman, breaking cultural barriers and societal norms in order to share the living water of eternal life. Through this interaction, the woman's life is transformed, and she becomes a messenger of the gospel, inviting others to "come and see" the One who has revealed the truth about her life and offered her the peace that can only be found in Him.

This story serves as a powerful reminder that the peace of Christ is not meant to be hoarded or kept for ourselves; rather, it is a gift that is meant to be shared with others, regardless of their social status, background, or circumstances. As we meditate on the truth of the gospel and the transformative power of God's love, we are called to be agents of reconciliation, reaching out to those who are lost, broken, and in need of the peace that can only be found in Christ.

The apostle Paul echoes this sentiment in his letter to the Corinthians, declaring, "All this is from God, who reconciled us to himself through Christ and gave us the ministry of reconciliation: that God was reconciling the world to himself in Christ, not counting people's sins against them. And he has committed to us the message of reconciliation" (2 Corinthians 5:18-19 NIV).

These verses remind us that the peace we have received through Christ is not merely for our own benefit; it is a sacred trust, a message of reconciliation that we are called to share with the world around us. As we embrace the practice of godly meditation and allow the truth of the gospel to permeate every aspect of our lives, we become ambassadors of God's peace, carrying His message of hope and redemption to those who have yet to experience the transformative power of His love.

Prayer:
Lord Jesus, we come before you with grateful hearts, acknowledging the incredible privilege of being called to share the peace of your gospel with a world that is often consumed by conflict, fear, and brokenness. We confess that too often, we have kept the light of your truth hidden, failing to be the ambassadors of reconciliation that you have called us to be. Forgive us for the times when we have been silent or complacent in the face of opportunity, and renew within us a sense of urgency and compassion for those who have yet to experience the fullness of your peace. Equip us, Lord, with the courage and wisdom to share your message of hope and redemption, reaching out to the marginalized, the oppressed, and the forgotten with the transformative power of your love. May our lives be a living testimony to the peace that can only be found in you, and may our words and actions draw others into the embrace of your eternal kingdom. In your precious name, we pray. Amen.

As we seek to share the peace of Christ with others, it is essential that we approach this calling with a spirit of humility, compassion, and authenticity. The world is often skeptical of empty platitudes or shallow expressions of faith, and it is only through the genuine manifestation of God's love and peace in our lives that we can truly make an impact.

The book of Colossians offers this exhortation: "Let the peace of Christ rule in your hearts, since as members of one body you were called to peace. And be thankful" (Colossians 3:15 NIV). This verse reminds us that the peace of Christ must first take root in our own hearts before we can effectively share it with others. As we meditate on the truth of the gospel and allow the Holy Spirit to transform us from the inside out, our lives will begin to radiate the very peace that we seek to share with the world around us.

Consider the example of the apostle Paul, whose life was radically transformed by an encounter with the risen Christ on the road to Damascus (Acts 9:1-19). After this profound experience, Paul became a tireless ambassador of the gospel, sharing the peace and reconciliation of Christ with anyone who would listen, regardless of their background or circumstances.

Yet, it was not merely Paul's words that carried weight; it was the authentic transformation of his life, the peace and joy that radiated from his very being, that drew others to the truth of the gospel message. His willingness to suffer for the sake of Christ, his unwavering commitment to the ministry of reconciliation, and his deep love for those he served all testified to the reality of the peace that he had found in Christ.

As we seek to share the peace of Christ with others, we too must be willing to embody that peace in every aspect of our lives. Our words and actions, our attitudes and behaviors, must all reflect the transformative power of the gospel, inviting those around us to experience the hope and reconciliation that can only be found in the embrace of God's love.

Moreover, the practice of sharing the peace of Christ is not merely a matter of words or proclamation; it is also a call to action, a call to be agents of change and ambassadors of reconciliation in the world around us. The Scriptures are clear that our faith must be accompanied by tangible expressions of love and compassion, a willingness to serve those in need and to be a voice for the oppressed and marginalized.

In the Gospel of Matthew, we read the poignant account of the sheep and the goats, where Jesus makes it clear that our treatment of "the least of these" is a direct reflection of our love for Him (Matthew 25:31-46). As we meditate on these powerful words, we are reminded that sharing the peace of Christ involves more than just words; it requires a commitment to living out the principles of the gospel in practical and tangible ways.

This may involve volunteering our time and resources to support those in need, advocating for justice and equality, or simply being present and offering a listening ear to those who are struggling with pain, loss, or brokenness. Whatever form it takes, our acts of love and service become a powerful testimony to the peace and hope that can only be found in Christ.

As we embrace this calling to share the peace of Christ with others, we must also be prepared to face opposition and resistance. The message of the gospel is often counter-cultural, challenging the world's values and exposing the brokenness and sin that pervade our society. Those who are comfortable in their ways or threatened by the transformative power of the gospel may react with hostility or rejection.

In these moments, it is essential that we remember the words of Jesus: "Blessed are you when people insult you, persecute you and falsely say all kinds of evil against you because of me. Rejoice and be glad, because great is your reward in heaven, for in the same way they persecuted the prophets who were before you" (Matthew 5:11-12 NIV).

As we face opposition and resistance, we can find strength and courage in the knowledge that we are following in the footsteps of the prophets and apostles who came before us, boldly proclaiming the truth of the gospel in the face of adversity. We can meditate on the example of Christ Himself, who endured the Cross for the sake of our redemption, and draw inspiration from His unwavering commitment to the ministry of reconciliation.

Yet, even in the midst of opposition, our call is to respond with the very peace that we seek to share. The apostle Peter reminds us, "Do not repay evil with evil or insult with insult. On the contrary, repay evil with blessing, because to this you were called so that you may inherit a blessing" (1 Peter 3:9 NIV). As ambassadors of Christ's peace, we are called to be a light in the darkness, offering hope and love even in the face of rejection or persecution.

Ultimately, the call to share the peace of Christ with others is not merely a suggestion or an optional component of the Christian life; it is a sacred mandate, a calling that is woven into the very fabric of our faith. As we embrace the practice of godly meditation and allow the truth of the gospel to transform us from the inside out, we become living witnesses to the power of God's love and the hope of His eternal peace.

As we journey through this life, may our hearts be filled with a deep sense of compassion and urgency, a burning desire to share the good news of Christ's redemptive work with those who have yet to experience the fullness of His peace. May our lives be a testament to the transformative power of the gospel, radiating the love and joy that can only be found in the embrace of our Heavenly Father.

And as we go forth as ambassadors of Christ's peace, may we boldly proclaim the message of reconciliation, offering hope and healing to a broken world. May our words and actions be a beacon of light, drawing others into the eternal Kingdom of God, where true and lasting peace can be found forevermore.

So let us resolve to be peacemakers, agents of change, and bearers of the gospel truth. For in doing so, we not only fulfill our sacred calling but also participate in the very heart of God's redemptive plan for humanity – a

CHAPTER 10

plan that promises to restore all things to their intended state of wholeness, harmony, and eternal peace in the presence of our Lord and Savior, Jesus Christ.

CONCLUSION

As we come to the end of our journey through the sacred practice of godly meditation, it is fitting to reflect on the profound impact that this discipline can have on our lives as followers of Christ. From the earliest pages of Scripture to the teachings of our Lord and the experiences of the apostles, we have been invited to embrace a lifestyle of intentional reflection, of quieting our souls before the Lord, and of allowing the truth of His Word to permeate the very depths of our being.

Through the practice of godly meditation, we have discovered a pathway to inner peace that transcends our circumstances and anchors our hearts in the unwavering love and faithfulness of our Heavenly Father. We have learned to meditate on the promises of Scripture, finding solace and strength in the timeless truths that have guided generations of believers before us. We have explored the beauty and majesty of God's creation, using the wonders of the natural world as a catalyst for worship and reverence. And we have been reminded of the vital importance of community and fellowship, as we have gathered together to share in the collective experience of meditation, prayer, and the study of God's Word.

Yet, our journey has not been merely an inward pursuit of personal growth and transformation; it has also been a call to action, a summons to be ambassadors of the peace that we have found in Christ. We have been challenged to share the hope and reconciliation of the gospel with a world that is often consumed by conflict, fear, and brokenness, offering a message of love and redemption that can only be found in the embrace of our Savior.

As we go forth from this experience, may we carry with us a renewed commitment to the practice of godly meditation, recognizing it not merely as a spiritual discipline, but as a way of life – a constant posture of attentiveness to the voice of the Holy Spirit and the eternal truths revealed in God's Word. May our daily routines be infused with moments of stillness and reflection, where we can pause to meditate on the goodness and faithfulness of our Lord, and find strength and courage for the challenges that lie ahead.

And as we walk this path of meditation and peace, may we never lose sight of the ultimate purpose behind our journey – to bring glory and honor to the One who called us out of darkness and into His marvelous light. May our lives be a living testament to the transformative power of the gospel, radiating the love, joy, and peace that can only be found in an intimate relationship with our Lord and Savior, Jesus Christ.

For it is in Him that we find our true source of peace, a peace that surpasses all understanding and guards our hearts and minds against the fears and anxieties that so often assail us. It is in His presence that we find our refuge, our strength, and our eternal hope, both in this life and in the life to come.

So let us go forth as peacemakers, as ambassadors of Christ's love, and as vessels of the Holy Spirit's power and truth. May the practice of godly meditation be our constant companion, guiding us, shaping us, and transforming us into the likeness of our Savior. And may the peace of God, which transcends all understanding, fill our hearts and minds, enabling us to navigate the challenges and trials of this life with unwavering faith, courage, and joy.

For it is in this peace that we will find the true fulfillment of our purpose, the realization of our deepest longings, and the assurance of our eternal destiny – a destiny that is secured in the love and redemptive work of our Lord and Savior, Jesus Christ, to whom be all glory, honor, and praise, forever and ever. Amen.

Made in United States
Orlando, FL
04 November 2024